D1083739

PAPER, INK and ROLLER

Print-Making For Beginners

by Harvey Weiss,

YOUNG SCOTT BOOKS

New York

TABLE OF CONTENTS

Thanks and acknowledgement are due the following museums, institutions, and individuals for their cooperation and generous help in the preparation of this book: The Metropolitan Museum of Art, New York; The Museum of Modern Art, New York; The National Serigraph Society, New York; Thomas Y. Crowell Company; Morton Kaish, John Ross, Clare Romano Ross, May Garelick, Seymour Chwast, Jason Berger, Maurice Sendak, May, Carla, Bill, John, Miriam. Illustrations, unless otherwise credited, are by the author.

Library of Congress Catalog Card Number 58-14993

Introduction

This book is about the kinds of print-making you can do at home with easily obtained materials. If you like to paint or draw, if you're curious about new materials and different ways of making pictures, you'll find print-making an exciting adventure.

When you make a drawing, you have only one copy after you're finished, but, when you're making prints, you can make as many as you want. You can make ten greeting cards, a hundred bookplates, or several big, colorful designs to hang on a wall or to give away as presents.

The book is divided into six sections. Each section describes a different way to make prints, and each section has illustrations by many artists, so that you'll be able to see in advance the kind of results you can expect.

If you've never done any print-making, start with the first two sections. They'll give you a general idea of the principles and methods of printing. Then, if you want to, you can skip around in the remaining sections.

Press Prints

If you put a little ink or paint on the tip of one of your fingers and then press your finger onto a piece of paper, you are printing! You are transferring ink from an object (your finger) onto paper, and that's the basic principle of printing.

The design on the opposite page was done in exactly this way, but, instead of using a finger, this design was made with a bottle cap, a tennis ball, the sole of an old shoe, scissors, a key, a seashell, and various odds and ends found in a tool chest. These objects were inked with red and black paint, and the marks, or *impressions,* that they made were combined to make a bright, colorful picture.

You can use nearly anything to print from—bottle caps, screws, a scrap of wood, a piece of sponge, an old fork. Look around and see what you can find. The next few pages will show you how you can print from these things and make your own designs.

RD FAMILY, by Morton Kaish. The original size of this press rint is considerably larger than this reproduction, as the case with a good many of the illustrations in this book.

6

MATERIALS: Collect all the different objects you are going to print from. Get a good supply of white paper to print on, some poster or tempera paints in different colors, and a few saucers to put the paint on. Cover your work table with newspapers, because you're probably going to make a mess.

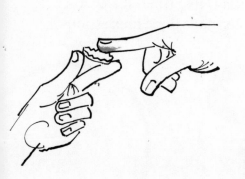

1. With a pencil or a stick, scoop some paint out of the bottom of one of the paint jars and put it on a saucer. For press prints you want thick, gooey paint, so don't use the thin, watery color from the top of the jar.

2. Pick one object for your first try—say a bottle cap. Dip your finger in the blob of paint and then run your finger lightly around the edge of the bottle cap to cover it with paint. Use a gentle tapping motion with your finger if you want a heavy layer of paint. If you prefer, you can use a brush instead of your finger.

3. Now press the bottle cap, paint side down, onto your paper. Press firmly and don't let it slip around.

4. Lift up the bottle cap. You will see that the painted edge has left its mark or *impression* on the paper. You've made a print! It's as simple as that.

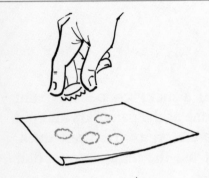

5. Repeat the process a few more times until you get the knack of it. You will find that you have to add more paint to the object before each new impression.

6. Now, make a print from each of the other objects to see what it looks like when it's printed. Can you tell what objects made these impressions?

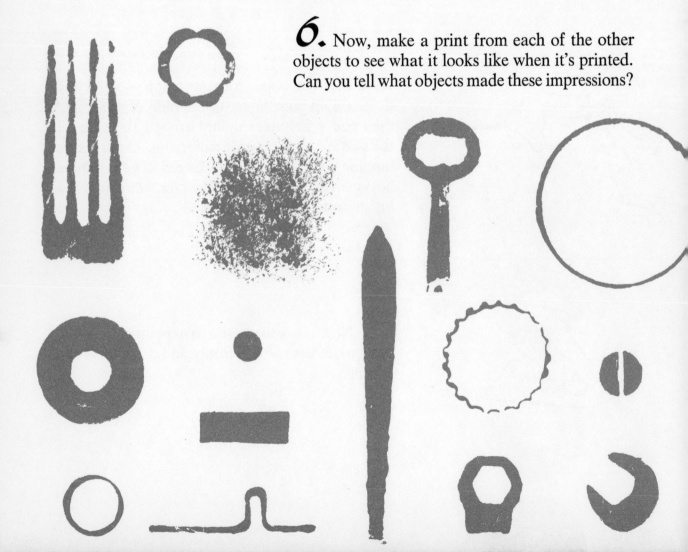

7. Try single impressions in a row, scattered around the page, bunched together, or overlapping.

8. Next, try different colors—the brighter the better. What happens when one color is printed on top of another? Try different combinations of colors and objects. If you want to print one object in several colors, wipe off each color before you put on the next.

9. For variety, you can take a strip of cardboard and print straight and curving lines with the edge of it. Try combining these lines and curves with the circles, squares, or dots that the other objects make.

Once you get started making a press print you'll find that many ideas will come to you. Try them out. You'll never know how good they are until you try them. Design is a matter of personal taste. As long as *you* like what you're doing, what you're doing is good!

The entire sheet of paper on which you print is the area of your picture. As you work, think about using all of this space for your design. After all, you want the whole sheet to look well—not just one corner or part of it. If you don't like the way your print is turning out, throw it away and start another.

A square, clean piece of white cloth can become a flag, a banner, or a fancy handkerchief. (Don't blow your nose in the handkerchief, the paint will come off.) A book jacket, fancy Christmas wrapping paper, a handsome design to hang up on the wall of your room—all these things can be made with press prints.

12

Transfer Prints

Transfer printing is the process of *transferring* the pattern of something onto paper. In this kind of printing the design has already been made for you, usually by nature. All you have to do is choose what you would like a print of and then print it. For example, if you decide to print a leaf, you cover it with ink and press a piece of paper down on top of it. The ink will transfer from the leaf onto the paper, making a print of the shape of the leaf and showing all its lines, ridges, and bumps.

Almost any kind of leaf will print well. If you use a big leaf with a rough surface, that's the kind of print you'll get. A lacy leaf will give you a delicate print. A fern makes a fine print. A few tufts of weed or some small flowers can look very beautiful, as the illustrations on the previous page show. If you want to experiment, you can make good-looking designs by using other materials, such as the bark of a tree or a plank of old weathered wood. Anything that is firm and that has a decided pattern and texture will print well.

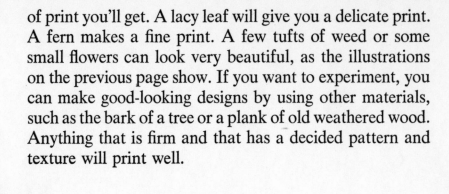

MATERIALS: For transfer printing you'll need a pane of glass, a spoon, newspapers, paper to print on, and the leaves or objects from which you are going to make your transfer prints.

A soft, thin paper is best for transfer printing, as well as for the other kinds of printing explained in this book. There is a paper called Japanese rice paper, which is ideal. However, not all art stores have it. Experiment with different papers until you find the kind that suits you best.

You will also need ink. You can get oil-base, block printing ink or regular printers' ink in black and colors in any art supply store. These inks come in a tube and are the best for transfer prints as well as for most of the other printing methods described in this book.

You will need some turpentine for cleaning up when you're through, because these inks are made with oil, and water will not clean them off your hands or clothes. Better wear old clothes when you print.

If you don't want to make so much of a mess, you can use a water-base, block printing ink. This kind of ink isn't as dark and rich-looking as the oil-base ink, but you can easily clean it up afterwards with soap and water.

To spread the ink on the object you're going to print you'll need a roller, called a "brayer" by printers. A roller does what your finger or brush did in the first section—it spreads the ink. A roller costs fifty or sixty cents at any art or photography store, or at a printers' supply house. It is a basic tool for most kinds of printing, so it's a good investment. You'll be using it for most of the printing described in this book.

If you can't get a roller, you can make your own "dabber" which is a pretty good substitute. With a dabber, you dab the ink on instead of rolling it on. This is the way Johann Gutenberg did his inking when he printed the first book. Instructions for making a dabber are given on page 20. But try to get a roller. It is easier to use and will give better results.

1. Spread some newspapers on a table and put the leaf (or whatever you have decided to transfer print) on top of the newspapers.

2. Squeeze a small amount of ink out of the tube onto the pane of glass. Run your roller back and forth over the ink in different directions until ink is spread evenly over a section of the glass. Now the roller is evenly inked and ready for use.

3. Run the inked roller over the leaf several times in different directions. Don't miss any of the corners.

4. Slide a clean sheet of newspaper under the inked leaf. (The other piece of newspaper will have ink all around the edges of the leaf, and you don't want this to print.)

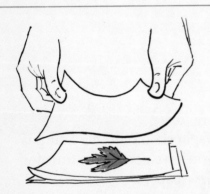

5. Over the inked leaf place a sheet of the paper you are going to make your print on. On top of this paper put three or four sheets of newspaper.

6. Now you do the actual printing by rubbing with a spoon on top of everything. The spoon will press the print paper against the inked leaf. Rub all over, up and down, round and round, back and forth all over the newspaper. Bear down hard, but be very careful to keep the papers from slipping. If the papers slip, the print will be blurred. No matter how careful you are, this does happen sometimes. If it does, just start all over again.

7. When you've rubbed all over, not forgetting the corners, remove the top layer of newspapers. Then lift up the paper you're printing on, and there's your transfer print. The print will have the exact shape of the leaf with all its lines, ridges, and textures. If your print looks light and gray, either you didn't rub hard enough or you didn't roll on enough ink. It takes practice to learn just how much ink and how much rubbing are needed. You may throw away a lot of prints before you get one you like.

8. After you've made your first print, put the leaf on a clean piece of newspaper, ink it, and print it again. You can continue printing the same leaf over and over until it gets too rumpled or crushed. Then you'll need another leaf.

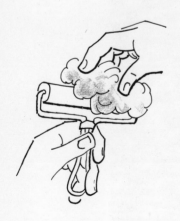

9. As soon as you're all through printing, clean off the pane of glass and the roller with some turpentine on a rag. Ink hardens in two or three hours, and if you let it dry on the roller it will spoil the roller. Be sure to throw away the turpentine-soaked rag when you're through with it. It's very inflammable and can start a fire.

After you've gotten the knack of transfer printing, see how many different kinds of leaves and grass will make interesting prints. You'll be amazed at the variety of shapes and forms you can find. Many small flowers and weeds will print, but anything very delicate may only last for two or three impressions.

See if you can combine two or more transfer prints on one piece of paper. Try using different colored inks. You might be able to print a bouquet! You may want to try printing on colored paper or combining a transfer print with a press print.

You can, of course, transfer print many different things besides leaves and flowers. Corrugated cardboard, rough sandpaper, or even a feather transfer well. To give you an idea of what can be done with a little ingenuity, on the opposite page there are transfer prints made from corrugated board, a feather, an old piece of wood, and a fish.

You can transfer print almost anything that has a rough surface. Sandpaper, for instance, printed in a light color will make an interesting background. Then you can print something else on top of this background in a different color.

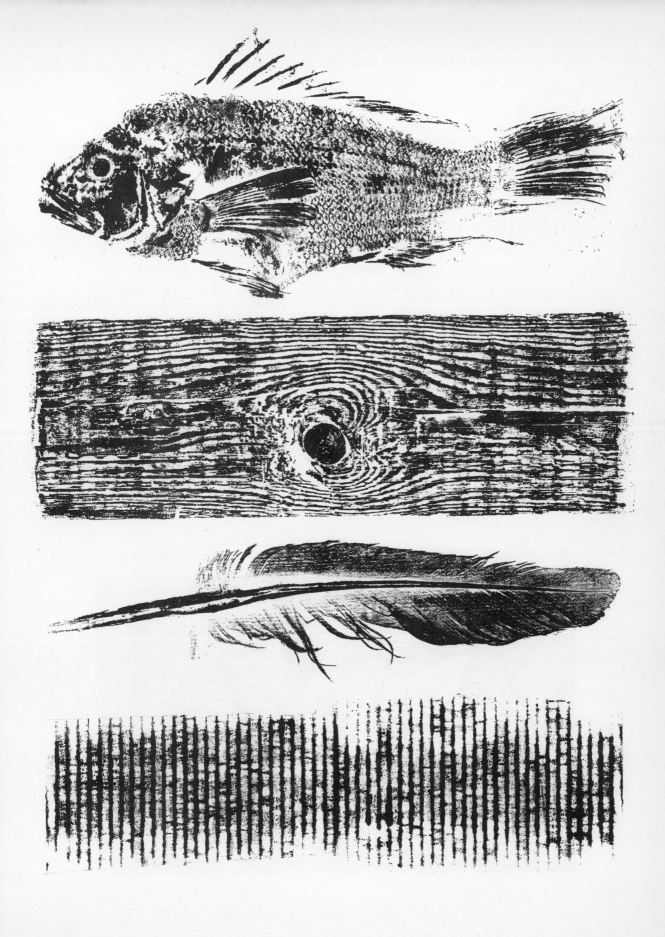

MAKING A DABBER: You'll need some clean, strong rags, some string, and if possible a thin piece of leather or suede. Roll a handful of the rags into a tight, round ball. Take a piece of cloth about twelve inches square and put the rag ball in the middle. Lift up the four corners of your square and tie a piece of string around them so that the ball is held firm. Add on six or eight more pieces of cloth. Tie each piece of cloth around the ball in the same way. Make sure there are no creases or folds in the cloth at the bottom because this part of the dabber has to be perfectly smooth. Finally, tie on the piece of suede or leather.

You can use the dabber instead of a roller for inking. You dab and rock it back and forth to get the ink evenly distributed.

A leaf printed with white ink on red paper would look like this.

Potato Prints

You can do more with a potato than bake it and eat it. You can use potatoes for printing. An uncooked potato is fine for making simple, bold designs.

Potato printing is based on the same principle as press or transfer printing, except, that now you have to make the entire design yourself, instead of finding it ready-made in the shape of a bottle cap or leaf.

In potato printing, a raw potato is first cut in half and the flat, cut side of the potato is used. The design you print is made by cutting away the parts that are *not* to print. The parts that are left standing up, or in *relief,* are painted. Then the inked potato is pressed on paper.

The potato print on the opposite page is made with one potato, printed in black and red. Color will do a lot to liven up your prints. It can help set a mood; it can make a print dull or bright, lazy or busy, sad or happy. But you have to be careful how you use color. If used too freely, color can make your prints look gaudy or garish.

23

MATERIALS: You'll need a good-sized potato, a carving knife, a small sharp knife, a small brush, some poster paint, and paper to print on.

DESIGN: Your design should be simple and bold. A raw potato is soft and somewhat watery. If you try to cut delicate shapes in it, it will break and crumble. Trying to make something precise and delicate on a potato would be like trying to write your name on the back of a postage stamp with a large paint brush.

Before you decide on a design, make several sketches on paper. If you don't like your first sketch, your third, or your fifteenth, don't give up. Keep trying until you're satisfied.

1. Cut the potato in half. Use the carving knife, because you need a perfectly level surface on the potato. Make sure the cut is straight and smooth.

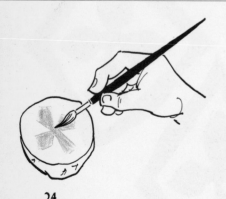

2. With the brush and paint, copy your design onto the fresh-cut face of one of the potato halves. Put aside the other half of the potato. You can use that if you spoil the first half or if you want to make a second print.

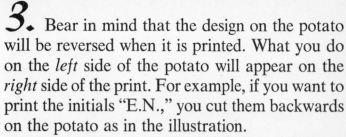

3. Bear in mind that the design on the potato will be reversed when it is printed. What you do on the *left* side of the potato will appear on the *right* side of the print. For example, if you want to print the initials "E.N.," you cut them backwards on the potato as in the illustration.

If you want to see how something is going to look reversed, just draw it on a thin sheet of paper and hold it with the pencilled side toward the light. You'll be able to look through the paper and see the design reversed.

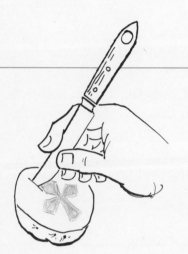

4. Now, take your small knife and cut away all parts of the potato *except* those parts that are painted with your design. Work slowly and carefully. You don't have to cut very deeply—a quarter of an inch is plenty. The areas which you cut away will make no impression on the paper when you print. They will appear white.

5. Take a good look at what you have. You may want to make some changes. If you don't like what you've done, slice off the face of the potato and start again. An artist is permitted to change his mind as often as he likes, or as long as he has potatoes!

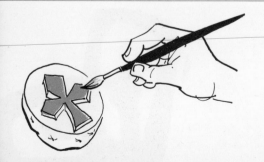

6. If you're satisfied with the looks of your potato, paint the raised parts. Go over them once or twice, but don't put on so much paint that it runs.

7. The next step is the actual printing. Place the paper you are going to print on top of several layers of newspaper. Put the inked potato, face down, on top of the paper and press down on the potato—not too hard or you'll end up with mashed potatoes, not too lightly or you'll end up with a light impression.

8. Now lift the potato and you have your first print! Looks terrible, doesn't it? Well, the first few prints are always gray and smudgy and not much to look at. Don't be disappointed. It usually takes several tries before the potato surface absorbs enough paint to print properly. And it also takes a little experimenting and practice until you get the "feel" of it.

9. Try a few more impressions. Remember that the potato has to be inked before every impression. When you get a good print, look at it to see if there is any way you can improve it. You may want to trim a ragged edge on the potato, shorten or eliminate something, or round a corner. You might want to add something, but that's one thing you can't do. Once you've cut off a piece of potato, there's no way to put it back on.

When you get a clean, neat print you can stop right there, but you'll have something much more interesting if you make a "repeat" pattern. That means one impression is made near or next to another on the same sheet of paper to make a large, over-all pattern. It's surprising how even the simplest little print suddenly comes to life when you repeat it several times—especially if you print it in different colors.

Space the prints in different ways. You may even want to turn some sideways or make them smudgy. Use all kinds of colors.

Some of the Japanese printmakers have made prints using sixteen or more colors, but the colors are always soft and fit into the mood of the picture.

Try making two different potato designs and printing them in different colors. See what happens when the colors overlap. Try printing on different kinds of paper—colored paper, wrapping paper, rough paper, smooth paper. In fact, try out whatever ideas come to you. You'll never know if your ideas are any good unless you try them.

If you want to print on cloth, the best material to use is cotton, and you will also need some of the inks which are especially made for this purpose. Ask for "fabric printing ink" at the art store. It comes in all colors and works very well.

A colorful potato print can be pretty enough to hang on anyone's wall. Potato prints also make fine greeting cards. A small Christmas tree design, for example, is easy to make. So is a snowflake or a star. Print on a paper of good quality—perhaps colored paper—and then fold it in half. Make your print on one page. Letter in "Merry Christmas" or "Happy Birthday" or anything you like on the inside, and you have an elegant greeting card indeed.

You can print a potato print pattern on cloth and cut up the cloth to make place mats. You can make a fancy tie, decorate an old "T" shirt, or make printed curtains for your room.

Stencil Prints

If you were to put a thin slice of Swiss cheese on a piece of paper and brush over the cheese with paint, you would be making a stencil print.

When you picked up the cheese you would find a pattern of dots and shapes on the paper where the ink came through the holes in the cheese.

This is the principle of stencil printing, but instead of cheese you use a heavy paper in which you cut out your own design. The paint that is brushed or sprayed on the stencil paper goes

through these cut out parts to the paper underneath.

As you can see from this description, stencil printing is exactly the opposite of potato printing. The parts that are cut out of a stencil *do* print, while the parts that were cut off the potato *don't* print.

The squad of soldiers at the top of this page was made with one stencil printed six times on a single sheet of paper. After each printing the stencil was shifted and a different color was used. The horses on the next page were made in the same way.

MATERIALS: You can get an oily paper which is specially made for stencils at some art stores. If you can't find stencil paper, you can use heavy Manila paper, bristol board, or paper about two or three times as heavy as the paper in this book. You'll also need some paint (any kind will do); a brush with stubby bristles or an old toothbrush; and, most important, a small knife with a very sharp tip. Any kind of paper is suitable for printing on.

THE DESIGN: As you can see from the illustrations in this book, each kind of printing has its own special look. Potato prints look one way, press prints another, and stencil prints still another. When you make your design, you have to try to make it right for the material you are using. Simple, bold forms are easy to cut out of stencil paper, so try to make your design simple and bold. It will look better and be easier to make and print. Trying to make a lot of thin, overlapping lines with a stencil would be like trying to carve a bird-cage out of marble. The marble wouldn't allow it.

For your first stencil make a simple silhouette shape. A fish maybe? A head in profile? A boat, a tree, or a flower? Perhaps you can *invent* a shape.

There is something else you should know about stencils. You can't leave any paper remaining inside a cut-out shape unless it's supported. For example, the way to make a stencil for the letter "O" is illustrated in the margin. If you didn't have those three little strips, called "ties," connecting the inside piece of paper with the outside paper, the middle would fall out.

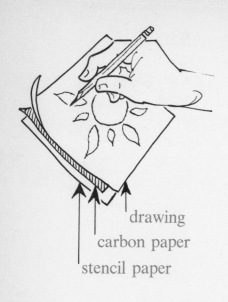

1. When you have a sketch that you like, trace or copy it on the stencil paper with a pencil. The easiest way to trace a drawing onto your stencil paper is with carbon paper. Put the carbon paper, shiny side down, on the stencil paper. Put your original drawing on top of the carbon paper. Then go over the lines of your drawing with a pencil.

If you have no carbon paper, you can rub all over the back of your original drawing with a soft pencil. Then put the drawing on the stencil paper. With a sharp pencil, go over the lines of your drawing. This will work almost as well as carbon paper.

drawing
carbon paper
stencil paper

2. Now you are ready to start cutting your stencil. Put the stencil on a pile of newspapers or a piece of wood you don't mind cutting into, because the knife will damage whatever is underneath the stencil. Cut out your design with the knife. The drawing on the stencil paper is only your guide. You don't have to follow it exactly, and you may want to make changes as you work.

3. After you've finished cutting the design, put the stencil on a piece of your printing paper. Tape or thumb-tack them together so that they won't slip.

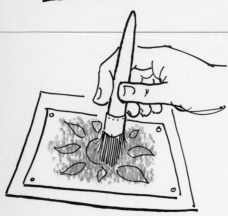

4. Now you paint through the holes in the stencil. If you're putting paint on with a brush, use very little paint or it will run under the edge of the stencil and blot. Instead of brushing the paint on, use a short dabbing or tapping motion.

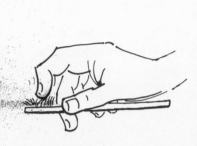

5. Another way to put the paint on is to "spatter" it on with a toothbrush. This way is fun, and it makes a more interesting print because it gives the paint texture. Put a small amount of paint on the tips of the toothbrush bristles and then run your finger back over the bristles. A fine spatter of color will be thrown off, making a pleasant, even tone. You can vary the depth of the tone by the amount of paint you spatter on. With a little practice, you'll be able to direct and control it easily.

6. After you have brushed or spattered the paint on, lift up the stencil. There's your design. If the edges of the print are fuzzy or blurred, you've probably used too much paint or the paint was too thin and it ran under the edges of the stencil. Wipe off the stencil with a rag and try again. It will probably take a few tries before you get to be an expert stencil printer.

Now that you have made your first stencil and know how to print it, you can do something else with it. Try repeating it several times on the same piece of paper. If you have a stencil of a tree, for example, and repeat it several times, you'll be able to make a forest! In the illustration below you can see what can be done with two different stencils—one of a man and one of a horn. They don't look like much all by themselves, but see what happens when they're printed several times in different colors and carefully spaced.

What would you like to make? A herd of yellow and purple elephants—with flowers printed on their sides perhaps? Or maybe you'd prefer to make a fleet of ships, or an *abstract* design?

The word "abstract" means to "take out of." You abstract the juice from an orange; you take out only what is important. The lower right-hand drawing is an abstract drawing. The artist has abstracted what he felt was important about two people bending over. Instead of drawing everything he saw, he has tried to abstract the essence of what he saw. Many modern artists work this way.

Stencils have many uses. You can stencil a border on a wall or even make a mural. (Before you start stenciling all over your wall, you'd better be sure no one is going to object.) You can make book jackets or posters. You can stencil fabrics to make curtains if you use special fabric colors. You can decorate furniture. Much early American furniture was decorated with stenciled designs of fruit and flowers. It's an excellent way to brighten up old bookcases and cabinets.

Suppose you are going to make a stencil of a goat like the one at the top of this page. When it is finished, there will be a lot of little pieces of cut-out stencil paper left over. These little pieces look like scraps, but don't throw them away. There is something you can do with them.

Put these scraps on a fresh sheet of paper in any arrangement you like. Then spatter black ink over the paper with a toothbrush.

When the ink is dry, lift up the stencil pieces. Where the stencil pieces covered the paper, there is no ink. You have white shapes on a spatter background.

That was just a trial run. Now do this. Arrange the stencil pieces on the paper in the shape of the goat. If you stretch his legs out, the goat will be running. If you slant his body and front legs upwards, the goat will be dancing.

Look at all the possibilities you have! By arranging the pieces a little differently each time, you can make a goat lying down, kicking his heels, standing up, or falling on his nose.

There are so many possible variations that some people enjoy working with the stencil pieces more than they do with the original stencil.

40

ROOSTER, *by Maurice Sendak.*

Cardboard Prints

Cardboard prints are made from pieces of cardboard. You cut the cardboard into shapes and paste them down on a base. Then you ink and print the shapes in the same way as you did the leaf in transfer prints.

The big elephant on the opposite page was made of thirty-six pieces of cardboard, cut out, pasted down, and printed.

The pictures on these two pages will give you some idea of the different ways cardboard prints can look. A design can be made with many small pieces of cardboard, or with one or two simple, bold forms. The rooster was made with only a few pieces of cardboard, but they were planned and cut with great care.

Making cardboard prints is a tricky process. You can get a handsome result or you can end up with something pretty sloppy, so follow the directions closely when you make your first print.

41

MATERIALS: You'll need a strong pair of scissors, some glue or library paste, printing ink, a small pane of glass, a roller, and a supply of paper to print on. You'll also need two or three good-sized pieces of cardboard—the kind that the laundry puts into a laundered shirt. (Page 14 gives complete information about inks and rollers.)

THE DESIGN: What subject will you choose for your cardboard print? If you don't have any ideas, that's understandable. You have to work to get ideas. You may get an idea by looking at the things around you—a tree, a bird, a dog, someone running, a truck, a view from your window. Any of these things can be worked into a good design.

Your design should be bold and strong. Avoid very thin lines. If you're going to make a print of a tree, for instance, plan it bold and black, like the illustration in the margin. And plan a fairly large print—anything smaller than five by five inches is hard to ink and print. You may find it helpful to draw your design with a thick black crayon or a large brush and ink.

Cardboard is hard to cut. If you try to cut out a complicated shape in one piece, the cardboard will bend and wrinkle. It's easier to make a complicated shape by combining a number of small pieces. You'll also find that a large black area, like a barn or the side of an elephant, will be more interesting if made up of several small pieces of cardboard rather than one big piece. The spaces left between the pieces of cardboard make a network of thin white lines and little gaps that is very handsome. This is one of the things that gives cardboard prints their special look.

Work for a variety of shapes in your design. See if you can combine large, bold shapes with small jagged, broken-up shapes. This contrast will give your print a strong, lively look.

1. Suppose you have decided to make a print of a tree. This is how you'd go about it. First, take a piece of cardboard a little larger than your drawing. This will be the base onto which you will paste the cut-up shapes.

2. Copy or trace your drawing onto the base. (Instructions for tracing a drawing can be found on page 34.)

3. Take another piece of cardboard and cut out a piece the shape of your tree-trunk. Put this piece down on top of the tree-trunk drawn on your base. This is a process of trial and error. It may not fit properly the first time. If it doesn't, trim it and try it again until you get the shape you want. When you're satisfied, spread the back of it with paste and press it into place.

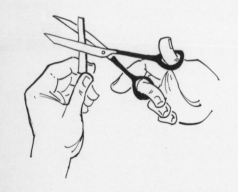

4. Now, for the branches of the tree, cut some narrow pieces of cardboard. Try them on the base drawing, trim them, and paste them down.

5. Do the same thing for the leaves. You may want oval, round, or diamond-shaped leaves. Cut them out and paste them down. As you work you may decide to change your base drawing. There's no reason why you shouldn't.

6. When you have all the cardboard pieces pasted firmly in place, you have what printers call a printing "plate." You are now ready to print. Squeeze some ink from the tube onto your pane of glass and run the roller back and forth over the ink to coat the roller evenly.

7. Ink the surface of the pasted-down pieces of cardboard with the roller. This is the trickiest part of cardboard printing. Go back and forth with the roller a few times in different directions. Use plenty of ink, but be extremely careful to keep the roller from touching the base. Small, isolated pieces of design are hard to ink without also inking the base. Ink them with a little ink on the tip of a finger.

If you get ink on the base it will show up as a smudge on your print. A few smudges here and there do no harm and may give your finished print a little variety, but too many smudges will spoil it.

8. When the design is inked, carefully place a sheet of printing paper over it. Then rub it with a spoon. You will have to do a lot of hard rubbing to get a good print. If the paper slips as you rub, the print will come out blurred, so hold the paper down with one hand and rub only a small section at a time.

9. When you've rubbed over the entire paper, lift up a corner and take a look. See if you've missed any spots. Is it dark enough? If it looks all right, remove the paper.

10. Your first print is called a "proof." Examine it. You may be a little disappointed because, like all first printing impressions, it's likely to be too light, too gray, and not quite the way you thought it would look. This is to be expected because it usually takes several impressions before the ink works its way into the cardboard printing surface. Sometimes the first proof looks gray because you didn't use enough ink or rub hard enough with the spoon.

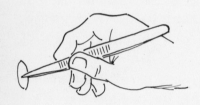

11. Now is the time for you to make any changes or corrections in your printing plate. If you decide to add something, it is a simple matter to cut another piece of cardboard and paste it down where you want it. If you want to remove a piece, pick it up with a fingernail or with a pair of tweezers. When corrections have been made, you can go ahead and print as many copies as you want.

You may have noticed that there are several prints of a goat in this book (pages 28, 38, 39, 50, and 60, as well as at the top of this page). If you compare these goats—each one made by a different process—you'll be able to see how the method of printing determines the style of a print. Even though the subject is always the same, the prints look quite different from one another.

If you're especially proud of a print, make a mat for it. A mat is a large piece of paper with a "window" cut out of it. It is placed on top of your print and serves to frame it.

To make a mat you will need a large piece of white board or heavy drawing paper. With a sharp knife and a ruler, cut a neat window the size of your print. Then glue the print to the back of the mat. If you make prints to give away as presents, put them in mats. Any print looks better in a mat.

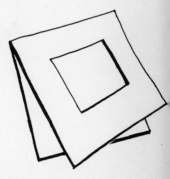

An illustration by
Henri Matisse for a book,
courtesy of the Museum of Modern Art.

An illustration by John R
and Clare Romano R
from MANHATTAN ISLAN
a book about New Yo

THE BATTLE OF VONCIO, *by Seymour Chwast.*

Linoleum Prints

The principle of linoleum printing is the same as potato printing. You start with the flat, smooth surface of the linoleum and cut away the parts that *don't* print. The parts that remain are coated with ink and pressed onto paper. But, while in a potato you have to keep your design quite simple, you can make almost any kind of design in linoleum.

A linoleum print can be as simple as the head on the opposite page, or as elaborate as the battle scene above. It can be a design of white lines on a black

49

background or black lines on a white background. It
can be small or quite large.

So many different results are possible because, although strong, linoleum is easy to cut. With linoleum
printing you have more freedom of design than with
any of the other printing methods described so far
in this book.

Linoleum prints have been made by four-year-old
children and by great artists. The print at the top of
page 48 was made by Henri Matisse, a famous artist
of our time.

MATERIALS: You'll need linoleum, cutting tools, block printing ink or printers ink, turpentine, rags, a roller, a spoon, a pane of glass, and printing paper.

You can get the kind of linoleum that's best for printing, as well as the cutting tools, at art or handicraft stores. Linoleum cutting tools are made with interchangeable tips which fit into a wooden handle. A simple forward motion of the tool scoops out a clean, neat, sliver of linoleum. You'll need a narrow tip for fine lines and details, and a broad tip for removing larger pieces of linoleum. The roller, ink, and pane of glass are the same as those described on page 14.

THE DESIGN: For your first attempt don't try anything too ambitious. Plan a small print with a few simple shapes—a fish, a rooster, a boat, a single figure, or a tree. Once you know how to cut linoleum, you can try something larger and more complicated, but your first print doesn't have to be any bigger than two by three inches. Make a few rough sketches until you get one you think you'd like to make a print of.

1. Copy or trace your design onto the linoleum. (Tracing instructions are on page 34.) Remember that the left side of your design will be on the right when it's printed. If you don't want it that way, you will have to reverse it now. This is how to do it. Place a sheet of thin tracing paper over your original drawing. Trace the drawing onto the tracing paper. Use a soft pencil and press down hard. Then put the tracing, penciled-side down, on the linoleum. Rub it with your fingernail or a spoon as hard as you can. This will transfer the drawing onto the linoleum. Your drawing will be reversed on the linoleum, but it will print the way you want it to.

2. Now cut away the parts of the linoleum which you do *not* want to print. Cut too little rather than too much. You can always cut away more after you've seen the first print.

When you're cutting always keep the hand that's holding the linoleum *behind* the tool, and always cut *away* from yourself. Then, if the tool should slip as you work (and it often does), it can't hurt you. This is a very important thing to remember.

Patience is a virtue in cutting linoleum. The linoleum will come off easily in smooth, even slivers if you don't try to cut out too much all at once. Make small, shallow cuts, because if you dig in too deeply the cut will have a ragged edge.

There may be some tiny little pieces of linoleum left in the areas that aren't supposed to print. If there are, it's nothing to worry about. These little left-over ridges and specks will add interest to your print.

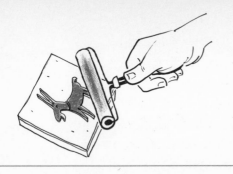

3. Squeeze some ink onto the pane of glass. Run your roller over the ink. Then roll the inked roller over the linoleum.

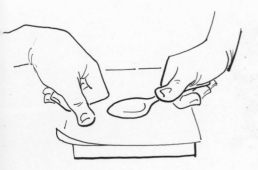

4. Take a sheet of paper and put it down gently on top of the linoleum. Rub the paper with a spoon, slowly, and carefully. Take your time. Press down hard and be careful not to miss any spots. Hold the paper firmly so that it won't slip.

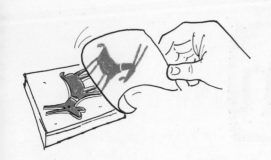

5. Now pick up one corner of the paper and see if the ink has printed clearly on the paper. If not, rub some more. Then, remove the paper and you have your print.

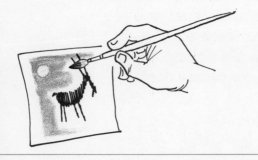

6. Color can be added to a finished print, either by hand or with a stencil or another linoleum block.

7. When you have finished printing, be sure to wash the ink off the linoleum, the roller, and the pane of glass with some turpentine on a rag.

Linoleum prints can be used in a variety of ways. They are perfect for almost any kind of greeting card. A big print will look well, matted and hung on a wall. If you make a small linoleum print with a little design and your name on it, you can use it as a bookplate. Make as many prints as you expect to have books.

If you make a small design, you can repeat it over and over again on a large sheet of paper. Then you can use the paper for book jackets, or even for wallpaper. (You can print a small piece of linoleum the way you printed a potato—just ink it and press it down hard onto the paper.)

A large piece of linoleum can be cut with a power saw into small squares. Then you can cut a letter, in reverse, on each little square and make your own printing type. Assemble the pieces to spell out a word (backwards), tie them up with a string, and print them.

CRAB, *by Jason Berger. The original size of this print is almost three feet square.*

Other Ways Of Printing

There are a good many other ways of making prints besides the ones already described. Most of these are quite complicated and require expensive, special equipment. But one day, when you've become expert with the techniques explained in this book, you may want to try some of them.

The next few pages will tell you a little about some of these other printing methods. There are no detailed, step-by-step instructions, but there are brief outlines of the principles involved, a few illustrations, and some simple experiments to give you an idea of what the results look like.

On page 64 a number of books are listed that explain these methods of printing in greater detail.

Woodcuts

You make a woodcut in the same way you make a linoleum print. The difference—and it's a big one—is in the material you use. Instead of cutting your design into relatively soft linoleum, you cut it into wood. Wood is hard and will splinter easily, so a good deal of skill and patience is required.

One of the nice things about woodcut prints is the way the grain of the wood will sometimes show up in the finished print. If a rough piece of wood with a coarse grain is used, the grain will add a nice touch to the finished picture.

Woodcuts are one of the oldest forms of printing. The first printed books were all made from woodcuts, the letters as well as the pictures. Each letter was slowly and painstakingly carved out of the wood.

On the opposite page are two woodcut illustrations for books. One was made at about the time Columbus was discovering America; the other only two or three years ago.

Coreizantes per annum

Ontigit tpibus heinrici iperatoris mirabile pɔ̈ instauditu. Lū iv villa ꝙdaz saxonie in madeburgēsi diocesi. vbi erat eccia sancti magni ꝙdā sacerdos missam celebraret in vigilia nati uitatis dñi. decem ꞇ octo viri siꝉ cū. xv. mulieribus i cimiterio ecclesie vbi celebrabat. choreas ducendo alta voce cantarēt. sacerdotemꝗ ipꜵ celebrātē impediebāt Mandat illis sacerdos. vt tacerent aut inde recederēt ꝙ sacerdotis verba deridentes. desistere no luerunt. Is amaricatus impcando inquit. Placeat deo ꞇ scto magno vt ita cantantes pmaneatis vsꝙ ad ānū corisantes. Et ita factum ēyt toto illo anno sine intermissione aliqua. corisando cantarēt. Mirabile dictu toto illo tēpe nec ros nec pluuia sup illos cecidit. Sed nec lassitudo nec fames

This is part of a page from the Nuremberg Chronicles, published in 1493.

n illustration by John Ross and Clare Romano Ross.

MITCHELL CORN PALACE—1905, *a silk screen print by Syd Fossum, courtesy of the National Serigraph Society.*

Silk Screen Printing

Silk screen printing is an inexpensive way of turning out a limited number of colorful prints. It is quite a new invention that has come into general use within the last fifteen years.

If you want to try an experiment, you can make a silk screen print yourself. You won't be able to achieve extraordinary results, but you will get a clear idea of how the process works.

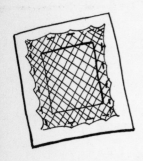

Make a simple silhouette drawing. Then cut a square window a little larger than your drawing out of a piece of cardboard. Get an old nylon stocking. Cut a square out of it, stretch it very tightly over the cardboard, and staple it in place. This is your screen.

Place the screen over your drawing and carefully paint a thick coat of shellac on the nylon up to the outside edges of your drawing. Let the shellac dry. Then place the screen over a piece of paper and spatter on ink in the same way you did for your stencil prints. Where there is no shellac, the spatter will go right through the nylon. But it will not go through those areas which you have covered with shellac. Remove the screen, and you have your print.

In actual practice, the process is more complicated. A rigid wood frame is used for the screen instead of cardboard, and special glues are used instead of shellac. Spatter is never used. Instead, thick paint is poured along one edge of the screen, and then pushed, or *squeegeed* across the silk. Because the glue, like the shellac, is waterproof and fills up the spaces between the threads of silk, the paint cannot get through these areas. But the paint does go through the silk where the glue has not been applied.

In a way this process is similar to stencil printing. In both methods paint or ink is held back by a "barrier." Paint or ink is allowed to pass through this barrier only in certain specific places. With a stencil, the stencil paper acts as a barrier, and paint goes through only where shapes have been cut out. In silk screen printing, a layer of glue on a piece of silk cloth acts as the barrier.

Because it is relatively simple and quick to prepare a silk screen, the artist often combines many colors in one print—although each color represents a separate screen and a separate printing operation. It is also possible to apply the glue so that a variety of textures appear in the finished print.

Silk screen printing is also sometimes called *serigraphy*. "Seri" means "silk," and "graph" means "writing." Silk writing. The word serigraph is used to distinguish between prints produced by artists and the commercial silk screen printing often used for signs and posters.

Lithography

This is a printing method based on the principle that oil and water don't mix. If you want to try a little experiment you can make a simple lithograph yourself.

Make a design on a pane of glass, using a wax candle to draw with. Make your design simple and go over every line several times with the candle, so that the wax line on the glass is heavy and bold. Then, lightly brush over the surface of the glass with a sponge dipped in soapy water. The water will remain on the glass, but it won't stay on the wax, because the wax is oily and oil and water don't mix. Now, roll some oil-base ink lightly over the glass. You'll see that the ink will stick to the wax, but it won't stick to the wet glass. (If a little ink does stick to the glass where it isn't supposed to, wipe it off with a piece of rag or paper tissue.) Place a sheet of paper on the glass and rub hard, all over with a spoon. Lift the paper and you have your print. The first print is usually poor, but later prints will improve. Be sure to sponge over the glass with soapy water each time before you roll on the ink.

This gives you a general idea of the principle of lithography. But of course a regular lithograph is somewhat more complicated to make.

Instead of glass, the lithographer uses a flat stone slab or a zinc plate, and the drawing is made with a grease pencil or crayon, not with a candle. The printing itself is done on a special press which exerts a very heavy pressure.

Because lithographs are drawn with a grease pencil or crayon, they often have a heavy, black look. The lithograph by Morton Kaish, reproduced on the opposite page is typical of the effect many lithographers

COLLOQUY, *by Morton Kaish*.

get. If you look closely you can see the marks of the crayon. In some places, like the arm and face, the crayon marks have been scratched away with a knife, leaving a white area.

The photo-offset process, very common today in book and advertising printing, is a type of lithography. It is the process by which this book was printed.

PORTRAIT, *by Albrecht Dürer,*
courtesy of the Metropolitan Museum

Engraving and Etching

With woodcuts and linoleum cuts, as well as with most of the other forms of printing described in this book, the parts of the plate that print are raised. This is called *relief* printing and is the method that was used more than a thousand years ago by the first wood-block printers, the Chinese.

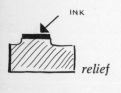

relief

lithographic

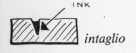

intaglio

In lithography, the ink is on the *surface* of the plate. But in engraving and etching, the ink which prints is held in grooves or trenches *below* the surface of the plate. This is called *intaglio* (pronounced in-*tal*-yo) printing. If you want to see for yourself how this process works try this experiment.

Take a small piece of linoleum and cut a few narrow grooves in it. Take a dab of printing ink or some paint on the tip of a finger and rub it into the grooves. Then, with a rag, rub off any ink that is left on the surface of the linoleum. Now, take a facial tissue, and fold it into a small square. Put it on top of the linoleum, and with a spoon, press it down as hard as you can. The pressure of the spoon will press the soft tissue down into the grooves where the ink is. Lift up the tissue, and you will see that the ink in the grooves has printed. You have an inked impression of the grooves, which appear as lines in your print. You have made and printed an engraving.

Ordinarily, engravings are made on copper instead of linoleum, and special tools are used to cut the grooves.

BLACK LION WHARF, *an etching by James McNeil Whistler,* *courtesy of the Metropolitan Museum of Art.*

Etchings are based on the same principle as engravings, but the method of getting the grooves into the plate is different. A copper plate is entirely covered with wax. The artist makes his drawing in this wax with a needle point which scrapes away the wax and exposes the copper. Then the plate is put into a bath of strong acid which eats into the copper but does not affect the wax. Wherever the needle has scratched a line into the wax coating, the acid eats or *etches* grooves into the exposed copper, similar to those you cut by hand in the linoleum. The plate is then removed from the acid, and the wax is melted off. Ink is worked into the grooves in the plate. The surface of the plate is wiped clean, but the ink that has gone into the grooves remains.

The paper to be printed is dampened to make it soft and pliable. It is placed on top of the plate and run through a press. The great pressure of the press forces the paper down into the etched lines in the plate and the ink is transferred to the paper.

Other Books About Printing

Some of these books are out of print, but most of them can probably be found in the larger public libraries.

CREATIVE LITHOGRAPHY AND HOW TO DO IT,
by Grant Arnold, Harper and Brothers, 1941

HOW TO DRAW AND PRINT LITHOGRAPHS, by Adolf Dehn and Lawrence Barrett, Tudor Publishing Co., 1950

HOW I MAKE WOODCUTS AND WOOD ENGRAVINGS,
by Hans Alexander Mueller, American Artists Group, Inc., 1945

HOW TO MAKE LINO CUTS, by A. Stewart Mackay,
David McKay Co., Inc., 1943

LINOLEUM BLOCK PRINTING FOR AMATEURS,
by Charlotte D. Bone, Beacon Press, Inc., 1936

BLOCK PRINTS, HOW TO MAKE THEM, by William S. Rice,
The Bruce Publishing Co., 1941

BLOCK PRINTING ON FABRICS, by Florence Harvy Pettit,
Hastings House, Publishers, Inc., 1952

SILK SCREEN COLOR PRINTING, by Harry Sternberg,
McGraw-Hill Book Co., Inc., 1942

SILK SCREEN STENCILING AS A FINE ART, by J. I. Biegeleisen and Max Arthur Cohn, McGraw-Hill Book Co., Inc., 1942

PRINTING FOR PLEASURE, by John Ryder, Phoenix House, Ltd., 1955

THE PRACTICE OF PRINTING, by Ralph W. Polk,
Chas. A. Bennett Co., Inc.,

GRAPHIC ARTS CRAFTS, by Désiré Kauffman, D. Van Nostrand Co., Inc., 1948

PRACTICAL ENGRAVING AND ETCHING, by E. G. Lutz,
Charles Scribner's Sons, 1933

MODERN METHODS AND MATERIALS OF ETCHING,
by Harry Sternberg, McGraw-Hill Book Co., Inc., 1949

S